Enable Me, Lord, to Shift

Are you stuck in idle?
Learn how to shift into
Truth and live!

Mental Domain

Book 2

By Darlene A. Larson

Enable Me, Lord, to Shift
Copyright © 2018 Darlene Alene Larson.
Author: Darlene Alene Larson
Product of Hearts with a Purpose.
www.Heartswithapurpose.com
Darlene@Heartswithapurpose.com

Author's note. I coach women. I teach women. In this book, you will read some of their stories. I have changed names, locations, and situations to guard their privacy yet tell their story.

Subjects: Larson, Darlene Alene/Inspirational Coaching Devotional for Women/Spiritual Living/ Christian Growth—United States.
Cover by: Taiwo David, Fiverr
Title: *Enable Me, Lord, to Shift* Are you stuck in idle? Learn how to shift into Truth and live! Mental Domain, book 2.

ISBN: 978-1-7335405-1-3
Printed in the United States of America

Acknowledgement

This book was written with the prayers and encouragement of many loved ones. And to all of you that have prayed for me or encouraged me along the way, I say, thank you.

Yet I want to especially thank my Hearts with a Purpose Advisory Board for cheering me on to keep writing: Robert Winter, Diana Luckhardt, Susan Loomis, Helen Blanchard, Debra Hinken, Phyllis Hoort, Sheri Felix, and Connie Van Houten. I could not have done this without your support.

And special thanks go to Helen Blanchard who spent hours critiquing my writing in the beginning.

And a BIG thank you to Pastor Robert Winter for critiquing my Biblical accuracy of each verse.

And thank you to my West Michigan Word Weavers group who read, edited, suggested, and affirmed me along in my writing journey.

And a BIG thank you to my friend, life coach, colleague, Cindy Tannehill, who believed in me.

And a huge thank you to my editor, Kathy Bruins.

And lastly, to my mighty Father God, I thank you and love you!

Dedication

I dedicate this book, *Enable me, Lord, to Shift*, in memory of my parents, Allan Kaye and Donna Terrell. Being raised on the family farm in mid-Michigan, I saw my father sow seed, and my mother sow love.

As I penned the devotionals, *Enable me, Lord, to Shift*, I reflected often of farm life, which includes planting time, growth time, and harvest time. In the springtime, my father would plow the fields, disk the fields, drag the fields, and again drag over the fields. This was to prepare the soil to receive the seed.

Once the seed was planted, it would take a few weeks for it to sprout. Weeds grew too. They desired to choke out the seedling. To kill those weeds my siblings and I hoed many fields row by row. After all, we wanted the plant to live, grow, and thrive. Then a harvest of corn, soybeans, wheat, and sugar beets would be the profit.

My father's sowing of the seed was like a foreshadowing to me to know how to sow the Word of God into my heart, one verse at a time. And it would take me time to grow. Plus, I needed to beware of the weeds that spring up from life.

My heart's desire for the reader is to receive the seed of Truth into your heart to live and produce a harvest from your life.

Contents

---------- ❖ ----------

Introduction

When I picture the word *shift,* I think of my first driving lessons. Like many other baby boomers, I was taught to drive with a stick shift. My dad's red Ford pickup was equipped with a stick shift—a long, skinny metal stick with a knob on top that came up from the floorboard. The stick danced a bit as you moved down the road. When I was driving, it was positioned to the side of my right leg.

In newer pickups, the gear shift was a lever located behind the steering wheel. The driver had to visualize the letter H to know how to shift. First gear was at the top left of the H. Second gear was at the bottom left of the H. Third gear was at the top right of the H, and reverse was at the bottom right of the H. If you never learned to feel for the gentle nuances between the clutch and the brake, the truck would jolt and jerk, and you wouldn't get far. And if you shoved the "stick shift" to the middle of the H, you went nowhere, even though the engine kept on running. That's called idling.

Later in life, I'd discover that learning to shift that old truck would be a lot like my journey through life. Like many women, I'd be tempted to remain stuck or push my way through the gears without learning the rhythms of the engine. My spiritual life would sputter, stall, and

1

get stuck in idle. Isn't that a bit like so many women's lives? We run, but do we get where we want to go in life?

Women's lives are full. Media feeds us false messages of who we should be. The fast pace of life leaves us harried and exhausted. Social media tempts us to compare ourselves with women in our church, community, across the nation and even around the world. We frantically scour the web, television, or shopping aisles searching for peace neatly wrapped in pleasure. In our efforts to run through life, we grind our gears and idle in agitation. We need to shift into another gear—to a life of freedom.

Enable me, Lord, to Shift is a series of inspirational coaching devotionals that teaches readers to examine each domain of their life. To change, we must look at who we are and then evaluate our life. We must embrace the good but also pull up the dead weeds to plant the seeds of Truth that bring about spiritual transformation and wholeness. The Truth is so important, and it's why I capitalize it through this book. Transformation takes time and practice. Only you can change yourself. I know because I learned these principles through the discipline of pain and personal practice. I invested my time, and the seeds that were planted years ago have begun to multiply.

I coach women. I teach women. In this book, you will read some of their stories. I have changed some of the names, locations, and situations to guard their privacy yet truthfully tell their story.

Enable me, Lord, to Shift, offers you a self-assessment report card, a verse, an inspiring story, and coaching questions to help you evaluate your life and align it with the Truth of God's Word. This book will teach you how to shift, from being stuck—to the truth to live a life of freedom and walk in your true identity.

I encourage you to grab your Bible and read each verse for yourself. This encourages the habit of opening the Word and personalizing the Truth. Then if you desire, mark, highlight, or underline the verse so you can easily find it again to refresh and revitalize yourself. Read the inspirational story, answer the questions, and close with the prayer.

Are you ready to make the shift? If so, the best time to begin is now.

BIG Picture Assessment

You will discover a BIG picture assessment in each devotional of the *Enable me, Lord, to Shift* series. It is a quick assessment. Once you read this book, and if you choose to purchase another *Enable me, Lord, to Shift* book, you will be able to compare your growth.

To know where to head, we must take an assessment of our status. We each are Queen of our own personhood, and God gives us free will. We run our lives from several domains in one day. A domain is a territory over which dominion is exercised, and you are the Queen of yours.

Synonyms to the word domain according to Merriam-Webster online dictionary: are *area, arena, department, field, Kingdom, precinct, province, realm, specialty, sphere, or terrain.* Circle the word(s) that you relate to. In this book, your mental domain will be the area of focus and growth.

First, please date your BIG picture assessment on page 6. Now, you need to grab some crayons or markers for this coloring assessment exercise. Please do not overthink this page. Keep it simple. I would like you to look at each domain, segment, or piece and quickly color or shade in how positive you believe that you are filled in that domain. The more color shaded means you are doing well. The less color means you are not doing too well. Start at the bottom line of each piece and color up. For example, your relationship with the Lord is in the spiritual arena. Color in how filled you believe you are in sync with God's Word.

Mental domain is your thought life. Is it healthy? Balanced? Positive? Wholesome thoughts? Or are your thoughts negative and critical most of the time?

Your emotions are your feelings. Do you control them or are your feelings running you over and out?

Physical domain is how you take care of your body and your surroundings.

Relational domain is your relationships. How are they doing? How are you handling them? Any toxicity growing in your life?

Financial domain is your finances. Budget. Tithe. Savings. Giving. Spending.

Vocational is your current career and life purpose. Passion. Purpose. Sweet Spot.

Quickly color in each area. Great job! Now, at the bottom of your page that you colored, please list in order the domains that you need to work on by looking at the colored pieces and the least amount of shading. Remember this is where you are at today. If there is anything else you notice on that page, please jot that down.

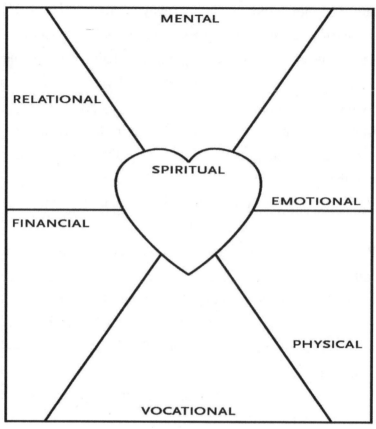

Date of assessment: _____

List in order the domains you feel you need to work on:
1. _____
2. _____
3. _____
4. _____
5. _____
6. _____
7. _____

Is there any new insight you gleaned?

Mental Domain Report Card

The mental domain refers to your thought life. Intellect. Brain-work. Cognitive processing. It's what you base your thoughts from and then grow your belief system.

What is right? What is wrong?

Who is right? Who is wrong?

What if we got to the end of our lives and realized we lived our lives based on projected lies and garbage others put on us, like post-it-notes? Crippled. Defeated. Lives of dead-end skeletons hanging on a pole. How sad and wrong. Yet the enemy, Satan, rejoices!

Take charge. You are your own thought-smith. It's imperative though that you take your clues and cues from the source of Truth. If it's not based from the Word of God, your life will be like a swinging bridge. Blowing in the breeze in every direction, but upright.

- ♥ Give yourself a current grade for your growth in the mental domain of your life _____
- ♥ What would you like your mental domain grade to be after you complete the 31-day mental domain devotionals _____?
- ♥ So, you understand, this book will only come to life, *if,* you practice the Word in your life and walk out the verses. What

would you like your mental domain grade to be *after* you complete the 31 devotional verses? _____

Today's date_____

1. Do you have control over your thoughts most of the time? Yes, No, Sometimes

2. How much control do you have over your thoughts? Circle the percentage

   1% 15% 30% 45% 60% 75% 90% 100%

3. Do you allow the words from others, their actions, or reactions dictate **too much** of your thought time? Yes, No, Sometimes,

   If so, name the people or the situations that **dominate your mind**. _____
   _____

4. Are their words (#3) or the ponderings of their words healthy for you? Yes, no, sometimes. _____
   _____

5. Do they match the Truth of who Jesus says you are? Yes, No, Sometimes

6. Who is in charge of what you think? _____
   _____

7. What will you do with the mistaken thoughts or limiting beliefs? _____

_____

8. Name one mental lie you would like to erase or delete? (I am too old, I cannot, I am not good enough, It's too hard, I am bad, I am a failure, I am stupid…) _____
_____What verse can you replace the lie with? (Psalms 139:1, 3, Phil. 4:8, Gen. 1:27…)_____

_____

I will sow the Truth into my life by taking this action step to argue down the lie to the Truth, as my reference. (Recite the verse aloud, write out the verse, memorize it). _____

_____

9. I will begin to change out the lie for the Truth by (date) _____

_____

10. I will tell (girlfriend, spouse, or accountability partner) that I am sowing this Truth _____
_____into my life.

11. I will review my step by (date) _____

_____.

12. By implementing the Truth, I will have and experience more

_____

13. I sign this report card, as I choose to take control of my thoughts. *Enable me, Lord, to shift mentally, thank you, amen!*

_____

Mental Domain Devotionals

Day 1

Enable me, Lord, to shift—my thoughts of accusations from the accuser to Truth.

Casting down imaginations, and every high thing that exalteth itself against the knowledge of God, and bringing into captivity every thought to the obedience of Christ;
(2 Corinthians 10:5 KJV)

Women's thoughts spin and tie into knots. If she is not slashing and slaying with the sword of Truth—lies begin to grow, disabling whole healthy living.

Where can you begin to untie the tangled thoughts? One thought at a time.

A thought demands entrance. You carve and cut your way through the pile of thoughts backtracking to discover the real source or the sender.

A wise woman holds the thought at bay in the pause-check-lane. If it aligns to Truth, she owns it and invites it to abide with her. If it is not Truth, she discards it, never allowing it to enter her mind and rob her of life.

Let's practice. *"I have no value. I did not get my "to-do" list completed. I am a failure. I cannot do anything right. I am no good."*

Whoa! We need to take one thought at a time to decipher where that statement came from. *"I have no value."* Is that true? It's a lie, discard. You were created in His image is the Truth.

Next, *"I did not get my "to-do" list completed."* Well, you had a full day and by not completing it, does that define your worth, your acceptance? Does the thought, *"You did not complete it,"* make you feel as if you failed? Maybe your list has *too much power over you.* Is this true, *"I cannot do anything right. I am no good."* Not true. The accuser wants you to beat yourself up. God's Word says, *"Cast down imaginations and every high thing that exalts itself against the knowledge of God, and bring into captivity every thought to the obedience of Christ"* (2 Corinthians 10:5 KJV).

Are you going to obey by bowing your thoughts to the Word?

- ♥ Are you stuck in self-defeating lies of your mind's chatter?

- ♥ Name the lie you choose to slay first?

♥ What Truth will you attach to the throttle of your mind, enabling a shift?

Enable me, Lord, to shift my thoughts of accusations from the accuser—to the Truth by bowing my thoughts to the obedience of the Word. Thank you, Lord. Amen.

Bow your thoughts to the Truth.

Day 2

Enable me, Lord, to shift—from looking into a cesspool of shame to looking to You.

They looked to Him and were radiant, and their faces will never be ashamed.
(Psalm 34:5 NASB)

I heard Jane's heart as she sobbed snap-shots of her story. This woman was stuck, and it was the lies of shame that kept her captive. She needed her life-line: her purpose.

She, like many women, longs for a purpose while trying to make some sense and order out of the stories of their lives. She shared of sexual abuse as a young child, an abusive marriage relationship, a miscarriage, being overlooked for job promotions, and the emotional pain. She added in a whisper, "I've been in counseling for years."

What does a woman do with a suitcase full of shame from her life? What happens when the sin of others spills over and sticks on a woman leaving its ugly residue of shame?

Often, women try desperately to shake it off by bathing those lies of helplessness and worthlessness in alcohol, food, immoral relationships, anger, negativity, or shopping. What do you hide behind?

Shame tells us, "You're the issue, it's you to the core of who you are, and you will never change." It drives in a stake of hopelessness. However, the Truth of God is for you. And He desires us to change our attitude and action.

To shrink the stronghold of shame, Jane began to slowly shift away from gazing at the cesspool of shame. She discarded lies, mistaken thinking, and shifted to embrace the Truth that she was not bad. She discovered God really loved her. She began to smile and laugh as she *looked to Him—and become radiant* instead of looking in the mirror of her old self-talk.

Together we met with her counselor, and he was impressed with her inner growth and positive progression. Counselor, coach, and client—all on the same team. Jane discovered that *her face will never be ashamed* as she *looks to Him.*

What are you gazing at to define your life?

- ♥ What is defining your life, the shame of the world or the Truth of the Word?

- ♥ Name the lies that hold you captive.

♥ Name one lie that you can uproot and then plant the Truth in its place?

Enable me, Lord, to shift from shame-based living to the Truth, as I look to You. Thank you, in Jesus name. Amen.

Jesus is my mirror.

———— ❖ ————

Day 3

Enable me, Lord, to shift—from impossible thinking to taking one small step.

Who dares despise the day of small things.
(Zechariah 4:10a NIV)

Life has dished out so much! Where do I start? I mean, really, is it the house, the kids, the parents, the in-laws, the job, my weight, my attitude, my anger, or my angst?

I lived this crazy out of balance way of life once upon a time. Dashing off to teach early in the day, scurrying back home to toss clothes in the washing machine, throwing meat in a frying pan for supper, sorting through the kid's homework piles, and then detesting those after-school phone calls, as if I needed one more thing to do. Then, to repeat it all the next day.

The Bible says the Israelites were told to take action and step into the Jordan River. They had to take the initiative by sticking their feet into the water if they were to cross that river. Likewise, a woman knows when her life is raging like the rapids. She must choose to take the load off her own back, one small step at a time. As Scripture states, "*who dares despise the day of small things*" (Zechariah 4:10a NIV).

As women share their daily list of "to-dos" with me, their voice volume shrinks as if sending a self-defeat message: <u>Impossible to live, really live.</u>

Women seek and long desperately to know where to begin. They are stuck on the fast track not knowing if, or when, they can stop—or if they dare.

Where to start? For me, it was stopping. I needed to stop and be still. My internal engines were close to blowing. Second, I knew I had to shift my career away from teaching children. So, with family support, I stopped, and dropped into a deck chair to pray, it was a *day of small things.*

As the Israelites began with one little step. I challenge you to do likewise. You can only change, who? You—what's your first step?

♥ When you hear the word "stop," what activity first comes to mind?

♥ Can you shrink the amount of time spent in that activity?

♥ When you hear "go," what one small heartfelt need do you want more of in your life?

Enable me, Lord, to shift from impossible thinking to taking action towards a small thing of Truth. Thank you, Lord. Amen.

Praise as you step.

Day 4

Enable me, Lord, to shift—from unanswered questions to knowing God saw the answer.

The eyes of the LORD are in every place, watching the evil and the good.
(Proverbs 15:3 NASB)

M any women lie awake at night riding the question carrousel. Questions spin through their minds: *Is my teenager having sex? How come she got the job promotion? Where were you God when my father abused me as a child? When did the cancer come back in my breast? Was my child aware that he was so loved here on earth? Is my husband viewing porn?*

Susie was one woman riding the question carrousel. Unanswered questions plagued her. And two, in particular, gnawed at her. Was her husband Davie aware of the holes in the storage room wall? Was he a voyeur or peeping Tom?

Susie's 18-year-old niece, Dawn, moved in with her and her husband three years ago because of Dawn's parents' death. Things started well, but Susie didn't like what she saw happening. Her husband seemed to be giving Dawn a lot of time and attention these days. And her husband of 17 years traveled for work. He thought it was fine that Dawn travel with him to job-shadow and be a good uncle-father figure.

Susie didn't like Dawn traveling alone with her husband for these business trips. However, Davie poo-pooed her concerns away. But Susie insisted that Dawn have at least a separate hotel room. When she found out that Davie had again ignored her request, alarms blew inside of her. She confronted her husband only to be dismissed.

A discovery broke Susie's heart. She had opened the storage room door to put Christmas decorations away when she noticed two little light rays beaming through holes in the wall, almost like headlights on a car. She walked closer to examine where were the little light rays' coming from? She gasped, you could look right into the next room. Her eyes peered into the bathroom shower stall. Her stomach lurched. This was the shower Dawn used. Was Davie aware?

Her questions were never answered. Their marriage collapsed months later. Yet not having answers was taking too much of her thought time and stopping her from stepping forward. I coached her and asked, "Is it not time to let go of the questions and surrender to God?" "*The eyes of the Lord are in every place, watching the evil and the good*" (Proverbs 15:3 NASB).

♥ Name your unanswered questions.

♥ Are any stopping you from moving forward in life?

♥ Will you shift, and hand your unanswered questions to God?

Enable me, Lord, to shift from the unanswered questions to trusting You saw it. You are God. Thank you, Lord. Amen.

God sees it all.

Day 5

Enable me, Lord, to shift—from anxiously looking at my circumstances to You my God.

Do not fear, for I am with you; Do not anxiously look about you, for I am your God. I will strengthen you, surely I will help you, Surely I will uphold you with My righteous right hand.
(Isaiah 41:10 NASB)

My heart twisted. My life was being exposed. I hated the public knowing. If I had ordered my life on a silver platter, I would have asked the Lord to please make certain I never ever had to taste three painful, yet pride-shattering dishes. First, to be a married woman and not loved. Second, to lose my home. Third, bankruptcy. Yet all three were coming to a head during the divorce proceedings.

For years behind the walls of my home, no one would listen to me. My words ricocheted around me. In actuality, they bounced off my then spouse and were not received, just like it says in Proverbs, a fool is one who chooses to neglect Truth and discipline. His actions rubbed my heart raw. They were polar opposite to my core value of being responsible.

The day I read my name in the newspaper in the foreclosure of my home my heart jerked. Then it broke into little pieces. How embarrassing? How irresponsible? I wept. Prayed. And spoke out—again to no avail. Soon, the house on the hill was emptied.

Have you ever encountered times when your voice was not heeded? Have you ever faced situations that repulsed you? How did you respond? For me, I had one choice, my God. *"Do not fear, for I am with you; Do not anxiously look about you, for I am your God. I will strengthen you, surely I will help you, Surely I will uphold you with My righteous right hand"* (Isaiah 41:10 NASB).

From packing to moving into a condo, to finding an attorney, to bankruptcy court, to Friend of the Court, to divorce court, to paying my bills, to growing my business, He led me. He strengthened me. He helped me, *I will uphold you with My righteous right hand.*

♥ Name a situation overtaking you with fear?

♥ Are you anxiously looking about?

♥ What shift can you make to look to Him for your Help?

Enable me, Lord, to shift from anxiously looking about my life to YOU as my source of help. Thank you, Lord. Amen.

He is with me.

Day 6

Enable me, Lord, to shift—from confusion to
You for peace.

For God is not a God of confusion but of peace…
(I Corinthians 14:33a NASB)

For a season in my life, I worked the front desk at an inn on weekends. When I wasn't greeting guests or answering the phones, the laundry room called me in. One Sunday evening while I folded towels, my mind flitted here and there. My thoughts landed on my brother's death. *He's gone, really gone—forever.* Only 40 years old and death had snatched him from us.

At times I think it's good to reflect. Like taking a simple one question quiz. *Am I living life fully and intentional?*

A guest arrived at the front desk. Interrupting my thoughts, I greeted and asked them how long their stay would be with us. The woman's voice caught. She said, "It might be longer than tonight. We don't know. We were informed six hours ago that our son is missing.

He was river rafting, and it's been 24 hours since they lost track of him."

I stood more erect. I said, "I'm sorry. What's his name? I will pray for him and for you." I finished checking them in and returned to folding the towels. I went to prayer.

One-minute life seems to be under one's control. Calmness. Steadiness. Sameness. And a phone call sends a parent's world into a field of unanswered questions that is chucked full of chaos, pain, fear, and tears. Or other "suddenlies" stampede through our lives. Death, accidents, tornadoes, illness, job loss, cancer, pregnant teen, or you name it. They are unannounced, uninvited, unwanted, sending chaos or confusion.

I heard the agony in this mom's voice. Saw the fear in her dark eyes and the tear-stained face of the father. Confusion abounded. *Where do you turn?* In 1 Corinthians 14, it says, *For God is not a God of confusion but of peace.* I folded another towel with vigor. Then prayed for their son and the parents. I promised to myself to live intentional while I sought the God of peace.

♥ Name one area of confusion in your life.

♥ What one thing can you shift to instead of the confusion?

♥ Did your peace barometer go up after you shifted?

Enable me, Lord, to shift from confusion to You, knowing you are the God of peace. May I purposefully shift to You, the Prince of peace. Thank you, Lord. Amen.

He is peace.

Day 7

Enable me, Lord, to shift —from no one is near to the *Lord is near to the brokenhearted.*

The LORD *is near to the brokenhearted and saves those who are crushed in spirit.*
(Psalm 34:18 NASB)

While driving, tears dripped and my cell phone went off. One hand on the wheel and the other hand grabbing my phone, I glanced to read the name. Coaching myself to keep driving, watch for traffic, and answer the call, I heard, "Darlene, Psalm 34:18, 'The Lord is near to the brokenhearted...'" I thanked him. Tears fell.

Why does life have to hurt so much? I bled of brokenness and hated change. My messy life was laundered for others to see. Home foreclosure. Bankruptcy. Divorce. Scattered teens. And I was transplanted to a new place called home. I reminded myself of the promises in Psalm 34, He *"saves those who are crushed in spirit."* And, *"the* LORD *is near to the brokenhearted."*

How is your spirit? Are you brokenhearted? Did you get some devastating news that is crushing in on you? Where do you turn? I began watching for God sightings remembering *the LORD is near to the brokenhearted.*

A few days after the cell call, I attended Carol Kent's Speak Up training. I bumped into Donna, a sweet friend. During a time of worship, we broke into small groups to share and pray. I spoke of my messy life. Donna prayed for me.

When we were leaving that day, Donna turned to me with a hug and said, "The LORD is near to the brokenhearted and saves those who are crushed in spirit." I was shocked to hear that verse coming from Donna's lips.

She had no idea that her husband had played a key role in my life. Her husband had recommended to a friend of mine the name of the counselor that I saw. It was my counselor who had called me on my cell phone to remind me, *The LORD is near to the brokenhearted.* God had brought this verse full circle through lives that overlapped then touched. *He is near to the brokenhearted.* Will you believe?

♥ Is your spirit crushed?

♥ Where are you turning for help?

♥ What shift can you implement to turn to Jesus?

Enable me, Lord, to shift from believing no one is near, to the Truth, you are near the brokenhearted. Thank you, Lord. Amen.

He is near the brokenhearted.

---------- ❖ ----------

Day 8

Enable me, Lord, to shift—from my thinking *to applying my mind to your knowledge.*

Incline your ear and hear the words of the wise, And apply your mind to my knowledge;
(Proverbs 22:17 NASB)

What does our mind manufacture? Our thoughts and we are the creator of them. But what if our thoughts stop us, derail us, and we use them to self-sabotage? What then?

For example, in high school, I took a typing class. Our lessons were timed. I hated that and panicked. I began to tell myself, *I couldn't type.*

Then in college, I had to type my papers. I shifted my thoughts to, *I am poor at typing, I'm slow.*

Fast forward a few years to when computers came off the assembly line. I tried my hand at the keyboard. It felt foreign, stiff, and uncomfortable. But teachers fresh from college brought their laptops

32

to school. They did their report cards on them. Impressed, I wanted to learn that faster method too. Could I learn to type?

So, I warmed up to the keyboard a little, then I left the school setting to teach my own children. My keyboard became my new chalkboard since I used an online curriculum at home. But I kept fussing. *I cannot type, and I type poorly.*

I sensed God calls to coach, speak, teach, and write for women. Trained as a coach, I began to listen well to my self-talk. Could my words be feeding my poor typing skills? I had a choice to make. Would I kick, fuss, and complain about my poor typing skills all the way through the writing of my books? Or would I change up my thought life? After all, Scripture states, "For as he thinks within himself, so he is," (Proverbs 23:7a NASB).

I began the hard work. I sat at my computer and said, *I can type. Feel your fingers on the keyboard. Relax. Breathe. Let them move across the keyboard gently. I can do this. Have fun. Enjoy. Type. I can learn. And even to type fast. Thank you, God, for helping me. This feels so right.*

Scripture states, *"Incline your ear and hear the words of the wise, And apply your mind to my knowledge"* (Proverbs 22:17 NASB). And that is what I did with Proverbs 23:7a.

♥ What thought are you saying that is self-sabotaging you?

♥ Name a first step you can do to eliminate that thought.

♥ Name a second step to change it up.

Enable me, Lord, to shift from my thoughts that stop me to your thoughts that enable me to soar. Thank you. Amen.

Speak Truth to yourself.

Day 9

Enable me, Lord, to shift—from being uncomfortable in new situations to knowing *He answers.*

In my trouble I cried to the LORD, And He answered me.
(Psalm 120:1 NASB)

Lucy was single and pregnant. She knew I was a coach for women and on the day that her boyfriend couldn't attend a doctor's appointment, she asked me to go with her. I met her. Then waited while she saw the doctor.

Lucy stepped from her room to the hallway. She waved me to come back. The doctor wanted to do an ultrasound since she couldn't hear the baby's heartbeat. My heart tugged.

What could I do to help this dear woman? She wasn't the mushy clingy kind. I looked her in the eye and said, "I am sorry, what do you want me to do?"

She said, "Go with me to the hospital." Ultrasounds, baby terms, a baby's heartbeat, this was all new territory for me. I had never conceived, and my medical knowledge was limited. But I knew the Truth. And I knew God saw this woman with me, and He knew if the baby was still alive. While she went for her ultrasound, I interceded for Lucy and her child, *"In my trouble I cried to the LORD, and He answered me"* (Psalm 120:1 NASB).

Then the ultrasound tech asked Lucy to return to the doctor's office for the results. She asked me to please go with her to her room. They informed her that the baby was dead. She would miscarry in the next day or two.

Once in the lobby, I asked if I could hug her. I said, "I am sorry for the loss of your first child." She received the words as her boyfriend walked in.

The next day I went to check on Lucy. She was in pain and had miscarried. She wept. Again, I asked God, *How do I comfort a woman grieving the loss of her child?*

I prayed, *in my trouble, I cried to the LORD, and He answered.* I made her soup, sat beside her, and told her I was praying. God showed me the way to comfort Lucy.

♥ How do you react in new situations or unfamiliar places?

♥ Do you allow the situation to take you over or do you stay on top of it in prayer?

♥   What can you do differently to add Truth into new situations?

Enable me, Lord, to shift from not allowing new situations to cause me to fear or be paralyzed in them and instead cry out to you to hear your answer. Thank you, Lord. Amen.

God answers.

Day 10

Enable me, Lord, to shift—from fear to a *sound mind.*

For God hath not given us the spirit of fear; but of power,
and of love, and of a sound mind.
(II Timothy 1:7 KJV)

What does fear do to our bodies? I came upon this verse, "*Men's hearts failing them for fear...*" (Luke 21:26). It caused me to pause; especially after reading medical reports stating fear can lead to heart attacks and I thought about my family genes.

Within a timeframe of three years, I lost my father and youngest brother to heart attacks, and another brother underwent a triple bypass. I visited my cardiologist for a checkup and was told, "My plumbing side of my heart looked good; yet, the electrical side wasn't beating in sync." He recommended medicine and a heart ablation. I didn't have peace with either.

Fear was all over the chambers of my heart knocking me down, robbing me of joy, peace, purpose, focus, and forward living. Even though I lived in a fear-breeding atmosphere, I was determined to shrink fear out of my life. When fear came knocking, I purposely chose this verse to wage war against fear: *"For God hath not given us the spirit of fear; but of power, and of love, and of a sound mind"* (II Timothy 1:7 KJV). I made a decision <u>not</u> to open the door to fear and allow it to march in, sit down, and start a conversation. I stayed alert and was proactive.

Three years later, I visited my cardiologist for a round of tests. Pleasantly surprised, the doctor told me my heart was beating at a normal rhythm. I knew who healed my heart beats through His *power, love, and choosing to keep a sound mind.*

Only God knew the inner heart workings of my father and brother. For me, fear had been a tagalong way too long. *"God hath not given us the spirit of fear; but of power, and of love, and of a sound mind"* (II Timothy 1:7 KJV).

♥ Where does fear attack your body? Headaches? Stomach issues? Backaches? Sleepless nights?

♥ What fear do you choose to shrink? Name it.

♥ What action step can you implement to face a fear?

Enable me, Lord, to shift from a spirit of fear to power, love, and a sound mind, knowing you are not the author of fear. Thank you, Lord. Amen.

Face your fears!

❖

Day 11

Enable Me, Lord, to shift—from refusing to admit I am a sinner to the Truth, *for all have sinned.*

For all have sinned and fall short of the glory of God,
(Romans 3:23 NASB)

S in. The word puzzled me for some time. Who sins? Do I? Do you?

We look to the Bible as the source of Truth. Romans 3:23 says, *"For all have sinned and fall short of the glory of God."* Once Adam and Eve disobeyed in the garden, they allowed sin to enter the doorway of the world. Everyone is born into this world a sinner, a broken individual, with a hole in their soul that causes one to lean into and love sin and to sin instead of turn to God. All have sinned. You. Me. Everyone.

41

Picture a newborn. For survival, their life depends on an adult, but by the time he/she is 18 months of age hands go to the hips shouting, "No." Who taught them that? No one. *I want my way.* A sinner they are.

Only God can be the change agent from sinner to saved soul because of His work on Calvary. A sinner bows their will and way to believe and receive Christ. His sinless body was sacrificed for you and me. He took our sins upon Himself. A gift of grace. God's riches at Christ expense. Have you received Him as your Savior? *"For all have sinned and fall short of the glory of God,"* (Romans 3:23 NASB).

So, what's sin? It is a transgression from following God and His principles. Adam chose not to obey God. Eve chose not to obey God. It's pride, do our own thing. It can be a thought, action, or not taking an action that is in accordance with the Word of God. Here are a few examples of sin that James tells us in chapter 3:14-17: selfish ambition, arrogant, lies, jealousy, and hypocrisy. A few more sins: fear, anger, worry, murder, adultery, gossip, coveting, idols, envy, loving false gods, not loving God, and many more. Scripture is clear that *"all have sinned and fall short of the glory of God"* (Romans 3:23). You are a sinner; therefore, ask Him to reveal your sin. He will. Then confess it and starve it out of you!

♥ Have you recognized that you are a sinner?

♥ Have you received the Lord as your Savior to forgive you for your sins?

♥ Name the current sin that sabotages your life. How can you shrink that out of your life?

Enable me, Lord, to shift my feelings that I am not a sinner, to the Truth I am a sinner. I recognize I am a sinner and need a Savior, Jesus. I believe and ask to receive you as my Savior. Help me walk away from sin's stronghold. Thank you, Lord. Amen.

Every human is a sinner.

Day 12

Enable me, Lord, to shift—from getting stuck on the word,
how to *the Lord knows how.*

*Then the Lord knows how to rescue the godly
from temptation.*

(2 Peter 2:9a NASB)

I tried to figure out *how* God was going to turn my life around. My overly analytical mind swung into full speed. I had asked Jesus, Creator of my life, at least a thousand different times, *how God?* And I flipped my thoughts over by the minute as if I was swinging in a trapeze show. The thoughts only multiplied fear and squished out the Truth, "*the Lord knows how to rescue the godly from temptation*" (2 Peter 2:9a NASB).

I asked God. And women asked me, *if I step toward my life purpose, then what? How* will my life purpose unfold? *How* will God provide for me? *How* will I write my books? *How* will I go back to college and not work? *How* will God lead me with my artwork? How? How? How?

I get it. The word *how* was my new BFF. Lord, *how* will this play out if I confront? Lord, *how* will you work out my finances? Lord, *how* will you bring me safely through to a life of abundance in peace, passion, and purpose?

The Truth, *the Lord knows how.* To shrink the power and control of the word, *how,* spend time looking up the verses of II Peter 2:1-8. Peter's writing tells us that God rescued Noah and his family. The Lord knew the *how* while the whole world was under a flood.

He rescued Lot, while the twin cities were under fiery skies of brimstone. The Lord knew the *how*. And if you are a godly person, meaning you love Jesus, and you choose to live for Him, then this is a promise keeper. He is your God, the same God of Noah and Lot. He knew the *how* then, and He knows ***the how*** now.

♥ What topic is it that you keep asking, *how Lord?*

♥ Name the area that you are to step toward in faith instead of being stuck in the, *how Lord?*

♥ I will memorize this verse by (date) _____.

Enable me, Lord, to shift from repeating how, to tipping my thoughts to the Lord knows how to recuse the godly man or woman. Thank you, Lord. Amen.

The Lord knows the how.

Day 13

Enable me, Lord, to shift—from comparing my life to others to compare my life to your standard, the Word.

For we dare not make ourselves of the number, or compare ourselves with some that commend themselves: but they measuring themselves by themselves, and comparing themselves among themselves, are not wise.

(2 Corinthians 10:12 KJV)

Comparison inched its way into my life when I was in my early teens. I had a friend that was my idol. She had the perfect figure, you know, the kind in the 70's where she was a #10. She rode my bus. And it seemed like every weekend she hit the mall because, on Mondays, the fashion queen herself had on a brand-new outfit.

Then there was Jane in high school. She seemed to get an A+ in English, in grammar, in vocabulary, in Algebra. I doubt she ever studied.

Then there was Nancy in college. She had such a lovely smile, confident, poised, and at peace.

Then there was Jan at church. She knew the Bible so well.

So who didn't I compare myself to? Yet, where did the comparing get me? It sowed in me an addictive thought pattern and an A+ in low self-esteem. And I had an elevated sensitivity to comparison for many years. Why?

Because I looked over at other marriages as a gauge. Mentally, I observed, listened, like the silent observer, yet all the time spinning questions. What was wrong with my then marriage? Why was it not going forward? I couldn't put my finger on the answer. Nonetheless, I had a sin stronghold of comparison.

By the time I got to my 40s, I was sick of the comparison sin. It left me mentally worse off. When I looked at my BFF's life, which was pretty darn good, I knew the sick game of comparison could destroy our friendship. I read, *"For we dare not make ourselves of the number, or compare ourselves with some that commend themselves: but they measuring themselves by themselves, and comparing themselves among themselves, are not wise"* (2 Corinthians 10:12 KJV). Convicted, I chose to stop comparing.

I aimed to become a wise woman. I chose to be intentional and to stop comparing. Whenever my thought life led me to glance over and compare my life to another's, I chose to **stop it!** Instead, I prayed for them. That cut the power cord to compare. Try it out! God's Word wins.

♥ Who or what do you compare?

♥ Are you sick enough of it that you will ask God to help you break free of this sin?

♥ When will you start this by?

Enable me, Lord, to shift to compare my life to your Word. Thank you, Lord. Amen.

Pray instead of compare.

Day 14

Enable me, Lord, to shift—from it's up to me to *God is a very present help in trouble.*

God is our refuge and strength, A very present help in trouble.

(Psalm 46:1 NASB)

Judy was a welcome sight to see in the school office. She had returned to teaching after the death of her husband. She radiated such inner strength of trusting God, and I admired her leadership. Yet, I'll never forget the question I asked her, "Judy, what is God teaching you through your grief?"

"It's a fog," she said.

Years have passed since this scene, and I have apologized to Judy for asking this question way too early in grief. I was overzealous in asking her what God was teaching her as I wanted to see how God had answered my prayers. Judy had told me to pray Psalm 46:1 for her shortly after her husband's death, *"God is our refuge and strength, a very present help in trouble."* And I had prayed many times for her that she would sense God's help immediately when she needed Him.

I have prayed this verse often for women. Whether they are going through labor pains, job changes, divorce, illness, teen turbulence, death of their spouse, death of their child, or other pain-filled tragedies.

Let us dissect this verse so you can own it as well. *God is our refuge and strength.* He will be there for you. A Strong Tower. A Fortress. And He will fortify you. He will enable you.

A very present help in trouble. Not to dismiss God or make fun, but this makes me think of something my mom always said when someone appeared right in the nick of time. *He is Jonny on the Spot.* Current crisis—God's aware. Future forecast—He'll meet you there.

He saw Judy in her grief, pain, and decision-making steps to know what car to purchase, house to move to, where to start a new job and meet new friends. He will be there for you too as God does not get tired nor run out of power.

♥   Name your present trouble.

♥   What strength do you need from God?

♥   How can He be your refuge?

Enable Me, Lord, to shift to you in times of trouble. Thank you, Lord. Amen.

God is alert to our needs.

Day 15

Enable me, Lord, to shift—my focus of sadness in grief *toward the Lord.*

My eyes are continually toward the LORD, for He will pluck my feet out of the net,

(Psalm 25:15 NASB)

At the care facility, my oldest sister greeted me. Then she updated me on our mom's status and handed me a devotional for that date. I started to read it, but my brain couldn't grasp the words. I asked her, "Would you please read it to me?"

My brain soaked in the words. And Deb read, *"The Spirit of God has made me and the breath of the Almighty gives me life,"* (Job 33:4 NASB).

Even though my mom was in a coma state, I knew her hearing sense was still in tune. And I imagined my mom smiling inside as she heard her eldest read to a younger daughter just like she taught us as children, *be kind to one another, get along, and love each other.*

My mom had only hours to live. And sadness and grief were grasping to suck me into a grief net. I had a choice to make. Psalm 25:15 says, *"If my eyes are continually toward the LORD, He will pluck my feet out of the net."*

Will it be, "stucksville" for me in the transitional shift with sadness in grief? Or will I keep *my eyes continually toward the LORD* which empowers and settles the uncertainty that spins with death, grief, and loss? I could not afford mentally to fall into the net of grief. I had to get through my mom's death and stay strong. Everything in my life was up in the air. And I mean everything.

Months earlier I had exposed my abusive marriage, and I was the evil one because I was a Truthteller. The house I lived in was in foreclosure, and I had days to be out. Which then would split the family unit. Literally, I was at a turning point in my life. If I allowed grief to wrap me up in its net, I didn't know if I could get out of it. I focused on Truth and chose to walk the Word out.

Where are our eyes to be gazing? What is my responsibility to own according to this verse? And for how long am I to do that?

♥ Where is your focus?

♥ Does your focus line up to the Scripture above?

♥ What step can you implement into your life to shift to focus on the Lord?

Enable me, Lord, to shift my focus from the sadness of grief and life circumstances to my eyes are continually toward the LORD, for He will pluck my feet out of the net. Thank you, Jesus. Amen.

My eyes focus on the Truth.

Day 16

Enable me, Lord, to shift—from denying the Truth to be Truthful.

> *The LORD is near to all who call upon Him, To all who call upon Him in truth.*
>
> (Psalm 145:18 NASB)

Betsy walked in, sat down, and said, "I am stuck." I normally begin a coaching session with a prayer as I want God's help through the Holy Spirit to coach. I asked her what she needed prayer on. She said, "My marriage."

Betsy had been married for almost 20 years. She learned recently of her husband's porn addiction when she asked him, *What was he viewing on his tablet?* She was grieved to the core of her being. (And women be aware too if you are viewing porn. It ruins lives. Get help—like now!)

Betsy shared how she wandered and walked from room to room in their home. And on one day, she sat on the floor and ate a bag of chips. She felt violated. Lied to. Betrayed. Used. Not good enough. Dirty. She said I *trusted him for all these years.*

I coached her to be real, "You are hurt, Betsy. All that pent-up pain wants to be expressed. Don't deny it. It'll send you into denial if you mask it. You're grieving."

"The LORD is near to all who call upon Him, To all who call upon Him in truth" (Psalm 145:18 NASB). And to be Truthful to God is mandatory. Since we cannot hide anything from God, even our pain.

I asked her, "What impression does this leave on you about your husband's porn viewing? How do you feel? What do you feel?"

"Honestly, I am angry. Hurt. HOT! Ticked. Frustrated".

I was proud of her for voicing. I asked, "What would you like to do?"

She said, "I want to talk, seek counseling and coaching."

Next, I had her vent by writing down her impressions and expressions from his sin-filled actions. *Anger. Sad. Worried. "The LORD is near to all who call upon Him, To all who call upon Him in truth"* (Psalm 145:18 NASB). Just maybe by gutting this all out in her rawness she might be able to stay out of the pit of depression.

What did Betsy want to do next? Betsy voiced. Betsy wrote. Betsy prayed. Betsy stepped right into a counselor's office and stayed on with coaching.

- ♥ What is it you need to be Truthful about with God?

- ♥ Name a hurt or hurts you have not expressed?

- ♥ Who can you talk to about this pain or hurt?

Enable me, Lord, to shift to speak the Truth of pain and loss to God and to others. May I be real. Thank you. Amen.

We are to be Truth tellers.

— ❖ —

Day 17

Enable me, Lord, to shift—from disbelief to remembering.

And they remembered His words.

(Luke 24:8 NASB)

Mary, Joanna, and Mary had just left the empty tomb. Shocked. Stunned. Disbelief. *Where was Jesus?* They had a quick thought choice to make, like a Y in the road of their mind. Which way would their thoughts lead them?

One way—disbelief. Shock. Doubt. Those thoughts waltz in creating chaos, panic, and fear, snatching away the Truth. Second guessing the man Jesus.

Or, the other Y in the road of their mind. Where Jesus had prepped and prepared them. Taught them. Spoke specific words to fortify them. I am Peace and the way of Truth.

Jesus knew this day was coming. First, the crucifixion and then to the tomb. And on the third day, He would rise from the dead, just as He said.

What about you and I? Are we any different than the ladies at the tomb? Our lives zip along. Jesus warned us too. We would have trouble here on earth. Read John 16:33. We deceive ourselves thinking we are in control and have the right to have it all. Then BAM and WHAM! A split-second decision to make. A Y in the road of our mind. Disbelief or *remembering His Words.*

I met Jane. She shared her issues. Her college-age daughter is sexually active. She fears she's going to have a grandchild to raise at this stage of life. Fear mounts. And her husband is working way too many hours. Her home is a disaster since she spends so much time meeting the needs of her young adult daughter. Her anxiety is climbing.

Where do her thoughts run off to? Can she or we slow the mind down enough to *remember His words?*

"He is your very present help in time of trouble." Read Psalm 46:1

"Fear is not of God." Read 2 Timothy 1:7.

"God is not a God of confusion." Read I Corinthians 14:33a

Jesus knows our day to day stories. He affirms that in Psalm 139:16. Will you and Jane choose to remember His Word?

♥ Which way do you want to pave your thoughts, disbelief or *remembering His words?*

♥ What is the first Truth you choose to remember?

♥ I make this split decision choice right now … I choose to remember God's Word.

Enable me, Lord, to shift to remember His words in split decision moments of life. Thank you, Lord. Amen.

Remember Truth.

———— ❖ ————

Day 18

Enable me, Lord, to shift—from believing that I am all alone to Your Truth, *I will never desert you nor forsake you.*

I will never desert you, nor will I ever forsake you,
(Hebrews 13:5b NASB)

Karen met me for an hour of coaching. At least ten times I heard her area of rawness, *I am all alone and so lonely.* I understand this loneliness ache. BUT … I think too many women cop out right here. They tend to believe their happiness is fed and fueled by someone else or something. It isn't, dear friend. We came into this world by ourselves, and we are going to exit it by ourselves. That does not mean we are to isolate, *oh no.* We are to live in community. But others are not to fill us up. So back to Karen.

What if she believed this verse, *I will never desert you,* which in the original Greek, this verse is written with a double negative: I will never, never, leave you. And I will not forsake you is written with a triple negative. I will never, never, never let you down. Pay attention my child, *I will never, never, never* ... Wow!!! Like three exclamation marks.

Let us go proactive to the positive. If we grasped the power of the indwelling of the Holy Spirit within, would we feel so lonely? After all the Holy Spirit is one of the Trinity. Which includes God the Father, Jesus the Son, and the Holy Spirit. We whom are saved, born again, Christian, in a relationship with Jesus, are not alone. NEVER. He abides within us. Like WOW, a constant BFF we could tap into and always be encouraged in the Word.

I know the fear of abandonment creeps into many lives. But I also know that many women are reading this whom have others in their space and yet, they are so lonely. Saying *I am so lonely* is enough to feed it, breed it, and multiply it. Don't be one of them. Invite Jesus into every domain of your life or go get counseling or coaching. "For He Himself has said, *"I will never desert you nor will I ever forsake you"* (Hebrews 13:5b NASB). Karen said it. Believed it. The Holy Spirit was within her, and the loneliness ache shrunk in size.

♥   Where in your life do you need to know that Jesus is with you?

♥   What can you do to receive this Truth?

♥   How can you marinate your mind in this Truth?

Enable me, Lord, to shift and thank you that I am not alone. You will never desert me nor forsake me. Thank you, Lord. Amen.

Holy Spirit resides within a child of God. Never alone!

Day 19

Enable me, Lord, to shift—from old thoughts to the renewal of my mind.

And do not be conformed to this world, but be transformed
by the renewing of your mind, so that you may prove what
the will of God is, that which is good and acceptable and
perfect.

(Romans 12:2 NASB)

Joy reached out to me to be coached. She wanted to know what
God's will was for her life. She had already tried reading her Bible
longer and going to church more regularly. She attended a new Bible
study and chose to work longer days at work. Plus, she got out of
bed earlier and added exercising into her life. She thought if she kept
adding new activities into her life that would change her. However,
her thought-life clicked the same ol' lies: *You cannot change. You*

are worthless. You have no value. You are such a failure. You are a loser. No one cares about you. Onward the lie gear cranked, running Truth right out. That led her into bondage of anger, anxiety, chaos, fear, frustration, jealousy, and worry. Exhausted, Joy felt old. Heavy. Rusty. Dead. Yet she was only 38 years old.

We went to work. Yet a different kind of work, *the renewal of Joy's mind* to the Truth of who God said she was. It took days, weeks, and months for Joy to shift to the Truth gear.

The mind is our control center. You are the controller. Think of our mind as housing two round gears. One gear grinds lies; the other grinds Truth. The more forceful gear grinds out the quieter or weaker gear. What you think on will dictate which gear overpowers, the Truth gear or the lie gear. *"Do not be conformed to this world, but be transformed by the renewing of your mind, so that you may prove what the will of God is, that which is good and acceptable and perfect,"* (Romans 12:2 NASB).

Eventually, Joy won over the lies that came from family traditions, culture, shaming, and fashion media. Now she can hear the Truth better and knows in what direction God has called her. After all, the Word speaks Truth.

♥   What lie are you sick of?

♥   What Truth do you want instead of the lie?

♥   Who will hold you accountable to sow Truth into your mind?

Enable me, Lord, to shift to the Truth gear. Thank you, Amen.

Renew my mind, Lord.

Day 20

Enable me, Lord, to shift—from participating in deception to expose it.

Do not participate in the unfruitful deeds of darkness, but instead even expose them;

(Ephesians 5:11 NASB)

This is a slice of a story from Cindy. She writes it for me to share with you:

We three sat at a funeral, and I was having my own private burial. The man that I sat next to had a condition that was eating away at his heart, surely as any cancer: S-I-N. She sat on the other side of him. And I wondered how much longer their relationship could be concealed?

This young lady that sat next to my husband at the funeral had his ear, but I didn't. Something was going on, but what? An emotional affair? At least. Yet, their relationship was wrapped in, she is just like family. *His words—not mine. People were led to believe this. Yet I*

68

wasn't allowed to have a say in her living in our home. No one knew yet that my voice was ignored. The emotional abuse was growing, and oppression was closing in on me. My private burial was to the death of a dream of a healthy and happy marriage.

Yet, I was accountable to God for my actions. I grieved and confessed how I handled my anger in reacting to my spouse and her. I hated the deception and the closeness of their relationship. My heart felt raped. And God did a major cleanout in my heart through repeated times of testing, trials, and tears. Broken, I grew out of my childish ways of reacting. I learned how to confront in Truth and kindness.

I thanked Cindy for sharing her heart, and I coached her.

Sin causes the heart to harden. If the sin is not dealt with, it claws its way into a life. Then it wreaks havoc casting off garbage bag-sized pain onto caring individuals. Innocent loved ones get caught in sin's casualties. Cindy had a choice to make, stand up for Truth or live a life of deception in a shell and say naught.

The Scripture says, *"Do not participate in the unfruitful deeds of darkness, but instead even expose them;"* (Ephesians 5:11 NASB)

She had been deceived and deceived. Cindy sought out help. Confronted. Exposed the Truth. Stood for the Truth. Sin addressed. Freedom came.

If your life is not based on Truth, then what? It's sinking sand.

♥   Is there anything you need to expose? If so, name it.

- ♥ Name your sin(s)

- ♥ When will you expose it by?

Enable me, Lord, to shift from deception or darkness to expose it. Thank you, Lord. Amen.

Confess. Expose.

———————— ❖ ————————

Day 21

Enable me, Lord, to shift—from focusing on life's changes to Jesus, who never changes.

Jesus Christ is the same yesterday and today and forever.
(Hebrews 13:8 NASB)

I had no idea how much longer we would all live under the same roof. The stronger I became as a woman with a voice, the more I was threatened and bullied. *You will have no heat, no cell, electricity will be cut off,* and money was already being limited to me for a few groceries.

It was imperative to keep recovering my mind with the Truth. I asked Jesus what I needed as a woman to survive no matter what would happen, and I checked off what I already had.

Check one—I had a strong relationship with the Lord.

Check two—I grasped to the core of my heart that my life did matter. God willed me to live.

Check three—God had created me for a purpose. His plan and way.

So what else did I need to survive as a woman? Security. Sameness. Stability. That's it! Women want something or someone that's stable, constant, and changeless. There is only one true source where true solid security comes from. Everything else in life will change. Everything. People, jobs, homes, bodies, children, you name it.

Whether divorce or death. Cancer or car accidents. Jobs or joblessness. Money or no money. True sameness or security is found only in Jesus. It's knowing and anchoring yourself to Father God who is changeless.

Hebrews 13:8 says, *"Jesus Christ is the same yesterday and today, yes and forever."* Jesus is the same, constant, changeless, loving, faithful Son of God. Day in and day out.

If I chose to anchor my thoughts on *Jesus Christ is the same yesterday and today, and forever,* I'd be alright. Notice the word**, *if*.** That meant if I focused on God and not on my marriage mess, the box filled with unopened bills, my children, or the house, Jesus still would not change on me. After all, He is my true security blanket.

♥   What is changing in your life?

♥ How are you handling it?

♥ How can you add Hebrews 13:8 to your life?

Enable me, Lord, to shift from focusing on life's changeups to You. Jesus is the same day in and day out. Thank you, Lord. Amen.

Jesus is constant.

❖

Day 22

Enable me, Lord, to shift—from believing I have no help
to *He is my Helper*.

THE LORD IS MY HELPER, I WILL NOT BE AFRAID.

(Hebrews 13:6 NASB)

I lived in a war. A deceptive war where words didn't match reality. I whispered three words more than any other in prayer, *Lord, help me*. And God helped me like a silent partner to navigate the landmines of the mind war I lived in. The abuser's words were targeted to take me out. But God and His Word were my ammunition, Truth.

The Lord helped me fight for my heart, mind, and soul to what is true, honest, and right. I sliced and diced the abuser's stories with discernment to get to the Truth or to the lie. I shook my head like an Etch-n-Sketch to see what words of Truth would stick and those that were lies evaporated. I kept learning, growing and understanding the depth of the abuse I lived in to become a sharp instrument of discernment and wisdom for the Lord to help other women.

God knew my future and my finances better than I. I pressed into Hebrews 13:6, *"The Lord is my helper, I will not be afraid."* I needed His constant help and to be reminded of this verse. I spoke the Word aloud. *God would help me if I were abandoned. God would help me if the kids stayed with me or not. God would help me if I didn't have a penny to my name or if I did. God would help me if I lost the house and needed a place to lay my head. God would help me tell the Truth. God would help me get on my feet. God would help me with my story and telling the Truth. God would help me write. God would help me grow my ministerial business.*

God would help me. He promised. He is truthful and faithful. I chose to believe Him. *Thank you, Lord, you will help me. I don't know how, but you will.* The word "how" was God's business. I was to obey. Walk by faith and not by sight. Do you want God's help?

♥ Where do you need God's help in your life?

♥ What do you want Him to do?

♥ What are you sensing that He wants you to do?

Enable me, Lord, to shift from believing I have no help to you will help me. Thank you, Lord. Amen.

God will be my Helper.

❖

Day 23

Enable me, Lord, to shift—from sinning to having sorrow
for my sin.

*I now rejoice, not that you were made sorrowful, but that
you were made sorrowful to the point of repentance; for you
were made sorrowful according to the will of God, so that you
might not suffer loss in anything through us.*

(2 Corinthians 7:9 NASB)

Jane, Ellie, and Betsy admitted they had issues. Their sinful actions had hurt others. They knew they must let go and let God take
charge of their life.

Jane struggled with anger, Ellie milked her physical pain for attention, and Betsy loved bragging about her adult children's lives. But
each of their love-hate sin reactions was not getting them what they
wanted out of life. Purpose. Joy. Impact. They knew they were made
for more. So, what were they going to do about it?

First, they each began to look hard at the consequences of their actions. Anger produced more anger, which added communication barriers for Jane and her loved ones.

Ellie's physical pain was an excuse to stop her from doing the tough stuff like exercise. And if she did not move her body soon, the pain would only increase.

And then Betsy with her bragging rights about her children camouflaged her empty shell. Bottom line … these women were self-centered, not Christ-centered. Sin had grown in each woman's life. Anger. Complaining. Bragging. Laziness. Manipulation. Jealousy. Boredom and purposelessness drove their reactions.

Yet each lady hated what she did. They prayed for godly sorrow, and in sorrow, they grew. Eventually, each woman stopped reacting in her sin-filled response and shifted to go after what she wanted instead.

Jane spoke calmly instead of reacted.

Betsy boasted about God's work instead of her children's. She began to investigate her purpose.

Ellie thanked God she could walk instead of complaining. She chose to go to a gym and get help and accountability. *"I now rejoice, not that you were made sorrowful, but that you were made sorrowful to the point of repentance; for you were made sorrowful according to the will of God"* (2 Corinthians 7:9 NASB) … and that is what brings lasting repentance, godly sorrow.

♥ What sin do you hate so much you are willing to let go?

♥ What do you want instead of that sin?

♥ Can you pray this verse into your life?

Enable me, Lord, to shift from sinning to hating my sin of _____ and having a sorrowful heart to repentance. Thank you, Lord.

Pray for Godly sorrow!

Day 24

Enable Me, Lord, to shift—from deception to
devotion to Christ.

But I am afraid that, as the serpent deceived Eve by his
craftiness, your minds will be led astray from the simplicity
and purity of devotion to Christ.

(II Corinthians 11:3 NASB)

"The Lord God commanded the man, saying, 'From any tree of the garden you may eat freely; but from the tree of the knowledge of good and evil you shall not eat, for in the day that you eat from it you will surely die'" (Genesis 2:16-17 NASB). Plain and simple, how specific God was, eat from *any* tree but *one*. Abundant provision. Faithful Father God. Trustworthy. Love. Peace. Goodness. Pain-free. Vulnerable. Joy. Order. Life.

Then came Satan's seductive twist: "Now the serpent was more crafty than any beast of the field which the Lord God had made. And

80

he said to the woman, 'Indeed, has God said, "You shall not eat from any tree of the garden?"' (Genesis 3:1 NASB)

Indeed, has God said, Satan questions God's Word. Next, he twisted Scripture, *You shall not eat from any tree of the garden.* He slithered in with a perspective of lack or not enough as if God was holding back. Satan cast doubt on the character of God.

Satan is a deceiver, a liar, and an enemy after our soul. The battlefield is our mind, and Satan has a strategy to claw his way into our thought life. He aims to have you doubt God. Then you don't trust Him. Paul warns, *"I am afraid that, as the serpent deceived Eve by his craftiness, your minds will be led astray from the simplicity and purity of devotion to Christ"* (II Corinthians 11:3 NASB).

The Liar deceived Eve, "The serpent said to the woman, "You surely will not die" (V.4). Eve listened to Satan. Then disobeyed the warning words of her loving Creator Master God. Her heart split. Destruction followed. Death arrived.

Eve had a mind. We have a mind. Eve had free will. We do too. Thoughts to think and choices to make. Will we obey or disobey?

Let's be wiser than Eve. Learn Truth. Listen to Truth. Shift your thoughts to be a devoted Christ-follower who obeys and practices the Truth.

♥   Name what you doubt about God.

♥   Write out the lie.

♥   What Truth can you replace it with?

Enable me, Lord, to shift my devotion to you instead of deception. Thank you. Amen.

Truth wins.

❖

Day 25

Enable me, Lord, to shift—from living in pretense *to confess my sins to another.*

Therefore, confess your sins to one another, and pray for one another so that you may be healed. The effective prayer of a righteous man can accomplish much.

(James 5:16 NASB)

I was 43 years old and tired of my emotional pain. Thankfully, God brought Susan and her family into my life at this time. They had moved into the area for her husband's new job. We met at a Bible Study. *I told her I had nothing to offer to her as a friend.* She mentioned *maybe it was time for me to receive.* Yet, I voiced what my life was like. *I was ignored, criticized, and negated. I was stuck in an ill marriage, needed for only one thing. I hated my life. And I disliked how the one female and her surrounding circumstances had been forced into my life. I was exhausted. Empty. Depleted.*

Never underestimate God's hands in friendships. By telling the Truth of my story to Susan, I was breaking the chain of abuse. Plus, I owned my own sin of pretense.

Susan gave me three gifts. First, she gave me time. Next, she listened to me. Third, she believed me. "Therefore, confess your sins to one another, and pray for one another so that you may be healed." Susan was the first step to freedom.

Women sit and spin in their secret sins. Stuck, just like I had been. They believe if I tell the Truth of my struggle, *they would disown me or not even be my friend.* But the Truth is the chain begins to break when we share our sin and/or what others have done to us.

Step one, confess, voice. It could be cutting, anger, hatred, rage, drinking, criticalness, pornography, abuse, or you name one.

Next, pray with that person who shares. And continue to pray for that person that shared their sin or situation.

And lastly, keep checking with them so freedom can ring. "Therefore confess your sins to each other and pray for each other so that you may be healed." And let me add on rest of this verse "The effective prayer of a righteous man can accomplish much" (James 5:16b, NASB).

♥ What friend or life coach can you share the Truth with?

- ♥ I will do step one by this date:

  _____.

- ♥ I will keep speaking the Truth and deal with my sin such as

  _____.

Enable me, Lord, to shift from pretense to tell the Truth of my life. I want to be healed from the inside out. Thank you, Lord. Amen.

Truth heals.

Day 26

Enable me, Lord, to shift— from believing love runs out to your love that is everlasting.

But the lovingkindness of the LORD is from everlasting to everlasting on those who fear Him

(Psalm 103:17a, NASB)

What do women want? The four-letter word: L-O-V-E. It's carved in barks of trees, on rings, and from the time we're little girls we hunger for it. Women want to know it. See it. Feel it. Believe it. Own it. That they're loved well, and men desire it too.

The issue is that women tend to believe this love factor will come from a man or a girlfriend relationship. Then they'll be fine and filled by another person's love. This is a problem though.

We're all human beings, sinners, broken and depleted. Our love runs out. It's fickle. Sometimes it's fuzzy and fizzles. You know, you hear, *I fell out of love, divorce him or her, be done, and move on.* Think again.

I coach and teach women until a person gets tanked up by God's everlasting free love gift, the Creator of love, the Source of Love. He/she will run out of love. We must be tapped into Him to receive love, feel love, and be filled in love. Then we can give it away. And God's love never runs out to those that fear Him and give Him their hearts, *"But the lovingkindness of the Lord is from everlasting to everlasting on those who fear Him.* Don't miss the ending of the verse, *on those who fear Him"* (Psalm 103:17a, NASB).

Do you fear God? Do you know God's kind of love? Do you sense His wholeness of love flowing through you and for you? You can. His love cements your being together. Solid. Secure. That's His motive of operation, to love you. Sure and steady. *"But the lovingkindness of the Lord is from everlasting to everlasting on those who fear Him"* (Psalm 103:17a, NASB). You are loved by a Triune God who made you.

♥ Who did you look to for love?

♥ Can you ask Jesus, instead, to fill you up to His overflowing love?

♥ Who do you want to love with God's love flowing through you?

Enable me, Lord, to shift from believing that love runs out to God's love is everlasting. Thank you, Lord. Amen

God is the infinite source of love.

❖

Day 27

Enable me, Lord, to shift—from a cluttered mindset to a *mind stayed on thee.*

Thou wilt keep him in perfect peace, whose mind is stayed on thee: because he trusteth in thee,

(Isaiah 26:3 KJV)

Sally craved peace. Her pastor husband was abusive. Verbal. Emotional. Drunk. She was stuck. Grieved. She read my blog. Emailed and we talked.

"Sally, what do you need?" I asked.

"Peace," she sighed and rambled, "He's telling me he's shutting down our checking account. He is accusing me it's my fault. He passes out at night. I am scared. The kids are scared. They do not want to be in their own home."

"Where do you want to start, Sally?" I asked.

"I am so exhausted. I am barely sleeping," she said.

Women get so confused in abuse. So scared. So very scared. It's hard to turn it off at night.

"I have never done this before. How do I live on my own?" Sally asked.

"I know the way to freedom, Sally. God will lead you. One day and one step at a time. I cannot tell you how God will lead you or how this will turn out, but I can tell you, God will lead you if you choose to trust Him. And God will provide for you too," I said. Plus, He says, *"Thou wilt keep him in perfect peace, whose mind is stayed on thee: because he trusteth in thee"* (Isaiah 26:3 KJV).

"Sally, what is your relationship like with God?" I asked.

"Cold," she said, "Even though I am married to a pastor, he told me I was being self-righteous and had no need to learn the Scriptures." And quietly she said, "I used to be a leader in a church before I married him. I also read my Scriptures before I married him."

I exhorted her to open her Bible. Take one verse like the one in Isaiah, *"Thou wilt keep him in perfect peace, whose mind is stayed on thee: because he trusteth in thee."* Memorize it. Sleep on it. Chew it. Eat it. Live it. Apply it. And watch the peace flow in.

♥   Where do you need to apply this Truth in your life?

♥ I will start memorizing this Truth by:

_____.

♥ I will say this verse aloud when

_____..

Enable me, Lord, to shift my mind to you and not the clutter in my mind. Thank you, Lord. Amen.

He is peace!

❖

Day 28

Enable me, Lord, to shift from believing no one understands to Truth, *You understand my thoughts.*

You understand my thought from afar.
(Psalm 139:2b NASB)

"How do I make them understand?" she asked privately through Facebook. The "them" was her girlfriends, and the woman was a worn-out widow with children. She desperately wanted her girlfriends to get her. Rally around her. Support her. Uphold her. Live life right beside her if need be, even in the pit to taste her pain.

A warning, women friendships can trip up right here. Self-pity creeps in, and women expect their girlfriends to become miniature gods. It's very dangerous to put that much pressure on a friendship. It cripples or destroys the relationship.

I was there once. I explained my pain over and over and over, yet my friend didn't get it or live in it. I knew I had to make a choice. I made a mental shift.

I was putting way too much weight on my girlfriend to be my buoy. She had a limited perspective. But I knew there was a man that saw it all, God. And I turned my thoughts believing, *"You understand my thought from afar"* (Psalm 139:2b NASB).

From that time on, whenever I cringed and cried and wanted a girlfriend or sister to crawl down to the depths of my emotional pain with me, I shifted. "He understands me," I said. Whether my friends understood or not, God got it.

Author Dee Brestin writes in *We Are Sisters*, "The healthiest change occurs if a woman matures spiritually and learns how to depend on God. She still treasures and nurtures her human relationships, but her dependence shifts toward the One who will never move away, betray her or die. Jesus is real—He is as close as your very breath." Will you let Him be your understanding Father Friend?

♥ What situation did you want a girlfriend to understand?

♥ Did her understanding fall short?

♥ What is it you want the Lord to understand?

Enable me, Lord, to shift my thoughts to you, the one who understands. Forgive me for any undue pressure I have placed on friendships. And if I need to ask a friend's forgiveness may I do so. Thank you, Jesus. Amen.

God understands me.

Brestin, Dee. *We Are Sisters* (Colorado Springs, CO: Life Journey, imprint of Cook Communications Ministries, 2006). page 23

Day 29

Enable me, Lord, to shift—from a counterfeit
life to the Truth.

If indeed you have heard Him and have been taught in Him,
just as truth is in Jesus,

(Ephesians 4:21 NASB)

I do life with myself day in and day out. Same for you, but it is you. Can we escape out of our own skin? No. Can you become me, or I become you? No. We look in the mirror. Put on our makeup, if we choose. Do our hair. Dress for work. Walk our day out.

What if we get to a point in life where we don't like doing life with oneself? We are the party pooper on our parade of life so to speak. If we get honest, we don't like what's occurring in our life. We might even confess, *we are a mess.*

I was there once. A major relationship in my life was closed off to others. I knew it had issues and voiced it to the other party. Yet it fell on deaf ears, and he negated it. The emotional pain was causing me to implode. The counterfeit way wasn't working. I could no longer pretend. I let go of enabling others, people pleasing, and the fear factor of, *what would people think?* I spoke Truth. I lived in an emotionally abusive marriage.

If we are a Christian and have received Jesus as our Lord and Savior, then we have the power of the Holy Spirit within us, who is Truth. And if we are living a counterfeit way, less than God's standard, the Holy Spirit will convict us.

Counterfeit means to reproduce something to deceive. Like Satan himself. These counterfeit ways or idols want you to acknowledge them, stroke them, and feed them, so they become your god.

For example, an unmet need arises from within. We tap into a counterfeit solution instead of running to Jesus. Whether it's porn, people pleasing, gluttony, gossiping, booze, boasting, sex or shopping, they trap us. They're greedy. Only Jesus satisfies. As the Ephesians verse says, "If indeed you have heard Him and have been taught in Him, just as Truth is in Jesus," let Jesus flow into every domain of your life. Then you might like doing life with yourself.

♥ Is there any counterfeit living going on in your life?

♥ Name the area or role?

♥ Name a step to where you can go to expose the lie.

Enable me, Lord, to shift from counterfeit living to Truth. Thank you, Lord. Amen.

Truth wins!

Day 30

Enable me, Lord, to shift—from my former manner of life, to *be renewed in the spirit of my mind.*

... that, in reference to your former manner of life, you lay aside the old self, which is being corrupted in accordance with the lusts of deceit, and that you be renewed in the spirit of your mind, and put on the new self, which in the likeness of God has been created in righteousness and holiness of the truth.

(Ephesians 4:22-24 NASB)

Daily Julie had to argue down the lies that she was going to fail. Her counselor, her doctor, and I cheered her on. *Believe Truth. Stay in the game. Live.* But doubts caused her to back step then sidestep. *Who's going to like my artwork? What if I fail? What if I cannot create anymore? The "what ifs"* dogged her.

Julie acted her way into her purpose. She stepped into her studio. She let go of one lie, two lies, and then three and crossed that great divide to Truth in her mind. Her mental gears shifted. She organized, cleaned, and prepped her space like warming her heart up to create.

The day came. Julie picked up a pen. Sketched. Used paint. She said, "Darlene, this is hard work. But I've never felt so empowered. It's me." She had retrained her mind to the Truth and died to the lies of the past, *"that, in reference to your former manner of life, you lay aside the old self, which is being corrupted in accordance with the lusts of deceit, and that you be renewed in the spirit of your mind, and put on the new self, which in the likeness of God has been created in righteousness and holiness of the truth"* (Ephesians 4:22-24 NASB).

Julie tasted victory, but fear kept hounding her. She invited me to her studio for a prayer coaching session. We prayed over each canvas piece. *God, please use her giftedness to reach out to the heart of the viewer. And even to those that don't know you, Jesus. Use her story of how she fought and clawed her way through the dark valley of depression and how you led her. Help her create and not fear. We thank you, Lord.* Unstuck from the old scripts of deception, Julie has her artwork on display in studios and shares her story.

♥   What is the first lie you need to let go off?

♥   I will step toward the Truth of _____.

♥ I will seek help for _____.

Enable me, Lord, to shift to Truth. Thank you, Lord. Amen.

Receive the Truth!

Day 31

Enable Me, Lord, to shift—from fantasy thinking and imaginations to your Word.

Finally, brethren, whatever is true, whatever is honorable, whatever is right, whatever is pure, whatever is lovely, whatever is of good repute, if there is any excellence and if anything worthy of praise, dwell on these things.

(Philippians 4:8 NASB)

I gave a devotional talk at a bridal shower. I desired to challenge the bride-to-be and the attendees with a positive challenge. I knew our thought life determined our outcome of our days. And I wanted this young lady's marriage to be successful. Plus, I wanted the women in attendance to recognize God had given us a detailed recipe of what we're to think on. I chose this verse *"Finally, brethren, whatever is true, whatever is honorable, whatever is right, whatever is pure, whatever is lovely, whatever is of good repute, if there is any excellence and if anything worthy of praise, dwell on these things"* (Philippians 4:8 NASB).

God used Paul to pen this verse in the book of Philippians while he sat in prison in Rome. Have you ever sat in prison? Dirty walls. Prison food. Stench. No windows. Temperatures that flux. Attitude that tumbles. Fantasy thinking and imagination run wild from sourness, sadness, self-pity to doubting God, depression, and despair? Goodness, I doubt we need to go to prison to experience any of these. Paul tells us we are to think on six-character virtues. If Paul could do this in his circumstances, in a prison, can't we? This verse is a command. God's recipe for a wholesome thought life.

First, marinate your mind in honest thinking. True. Reliable, like God and His Word.

Second, hover your thought life on topics that are honorable, dignified, and respectful in moral excellence. They invite reverence.

Third, click your thoughts to justice and conformity to God's standards of righteousness.

Fourth, drive your thoughts to purity, then park them there.

Fifth, steer your thoughts to love that they be pleasing with winsome ways.

Sixth, guide and guard your thoughts to positive, constructive, and fair-speaking which is attractive. Dwell on things that build up. Give a positive praise. Let go of fantasy thinking.

Perhaps, the young bride to be at the bridal shower applied this verse. Today, she is still married and happily!

♥ What thoughts do you need to flush out?

♥ You will do this by_____.

♥ Instead you will dwell on _____.

Enable me, Lord, to shift my thoughts to your recipe. Thank you. Amen.

Meditate on Truth.

———————— ❖ ————————

Wrap Up Time!

Congratulations, you have completed the mental domain book of the *Enable me, Lord, to Shift* series. My hope and desire are that you have made inroads to your thought life and allowed the Truth to take over more of your daily thoughts.

In closing, I would like you to take a pen or pencil and flip back to the BIG Assessment on page 6 that you shaded in over 31 days ago. Now, I would like you to draw a cross in the little heart in the center of the page. That little cross is to represent to you what Christ did for you and me. He was a perfect person yet God-man to die for you and me.

The cross you drew is to represent the freedom we have for the asking *IF* we apply the Truth to our life with the empowering and filling of the Holy Spirit. He will help you spread Truth into each domain of your life setting you free to live.

First, it begins with your relationship with the Lord in the spiritual domain. Next, I would like you to look at your BIG Assessment page and see which domains you need help in next? Is it the mental, emotional or physical domain?

If it were up to me, I would suggest you read the spiritual, mental, and emotional books in that order. But if you have read them out of order, no issue. The KEY is to apply the Word to your life and get practicing it.

Once you have read and applied the Word to your life watch how the freedom from the Truth will spread over into each domain of your life. Thus, you then can take your pencil or pen and go back to your Big Assessment on page 6. Draw the little cross lines longer and wider as your relationship with God spills and spreads over into every other domain, bringing God's Word alive in all areas of your life. God's way works offering you freedom to live!

Also, do not forget to go back and check over your mental domain report card.

One more closing comment, I love to stay in touch with my readers and be in community.

Please email me Darlene@Heartswithapurpose.com and tell me how the book changed your life. Also, join Hearts with a Purpose readers and sign up to receive the weekly complimentary coaching newsletter, free to you, at www.Heartswithapurpose.com. If you are in need of a woman's speaker for your event contact me. I love to coach, speak, teach, and write on behalf of the needs of women.

God Bless you friend, Coach Darlene Larson

The first three books in print are:

Enable me, Lord, to Shift, Are you stuck in idle? Learn how to shift into Truth and live!

Book 1, Spiritual Domain

Enable me, Lord, to Shift, Are you stuck in idle? Learn how to shift into Truth and live!

Book 2, Mental Domain

Enable me, Lord, to Shift, Are you stuck in idle? Learn how to shift into Truth and live!

Book 3, Emotional Domain

Each book is a product of Hearts with a Purpose. www.Heartswitha-purpose.com

CPSIA information can be obtained
at www.ICGtesting.com
Printed in the USA
FSHW010654120719
59827FS

9 781733 540513